# RAGES OF THE CARBOLIC
## CLIVE GRESSWELL

Newton-le-Willows

Published in the United Kingdom in 2019
by The Knives Forks And Spoons Press,
51 Pipit Avenue,
Newton-le-Willows,
Merseyside,
WA12 9RG.

ISBN 978-1-912211-33-3

Copyright © Clive Gresswell, 2019.

The right of Clive Gresswell to be identified as the author of this work has been asserted by them in accordance with the Copyrights, Designs and Patents Act of 1988. All rights reserved. No part of this publication may be reproduced, stored in a retrieval system, transmitted in any form or by any means, electronic, photocopying, recording or otherwise, without prior permission of the publisher.

**Acknowledgements:**

Some of the poems in this book have appeared in *BlazeVOX, Dispatches, A Glimpse Of, Tears In The Fence* and *Adjacent Pineapple.*

# RAGES OF THE CARBOLIC

# CONTENTS

Part 1: The (Bracket) Poems      7

Part 2: The Other Exploded      23

Part 3: The Tapes      45

Part 4: End Poems      55

# Part 1

The (Bracket) Poems

restless (breathing) font
candles simper summer
curling beneath passions
the lake (where) we
& the hurtling armada
fleet of foot & choosing root vegetables
(laughter) & where we fit
new shapes from this froth of form
a gate left partly open
to glimpsed
narrow (needless) chattering
divulging corners of winter
(we) crept into the crypts
& buttercup fields

imprison freestanding freeze clouds
deft upon the wind of calling
time-honoured what we issued
amazing departures from the alphabet
stringed instruments the pearls
& motifs on the t-shirts
he called back to you
on a trail of your destiny
theresa may will see you now
slipped from grace & disreputable
sit & dispatch these trifles
a confederacy of envelopes
cast soft upon the european mind
howlings/refugees/impinge
somewhere a burning question
seeps deep into your gut
the high command you swallowed

peeling back the worm
twisted over years
laughter & sweet nothings
treasures & rubble
sunk to the bottom of this ocean
among the coral & garbage
flags & banners flying
is there a future in it?
he watches from his tower
the holy prince of ego

time honours this restless
sea legs jostle
he plagued among your wildernesses
brings daughters into this world
some cannot speak
at least not in the classical sense
let their limbs litter
the darkness of this river
flowing with the blood-dark howlings
fledglings with their pamphlets
and hurry to the crazed indian
he tore up their terrible secrets
stole them into their dreams of night
made a pact among the seedlings
we'll guide you to the light

a tremendous gluttony of effort
in times the purple trail
he follows on the evidence
cast across the shores
his handsome siren calling
from lake to shore to lake
clasped in his fist a ring
of the world's first metal caste
but beneath the tower
sits this rusting nail of hatred
coiled on the spring
from which his watch was born
come in my child and feed us
alone & tattered & worn
in london's fair city

new feet tread (on)
corners of the old (mind)
& lifting up a carpet of shopping (malls)
dread feelings (locked) unpick (shocked)
like tiny shells
you witnessed in your (youth)
washed upon tradition's breech
giant strides (pass) on the other side
the places where the factories struck (down)
with a kind of influenza
tributes (played) on (this) marching band
a tower's locks (unpicked)
we panicked in the (deadly) night sin
cities wheeling (fire) among the birds
(they) peck (&) peck (&) peck again
time & his idle hands (unsullied?)
who can say where (jesters) lay
& who should go unpunished

the will of the people
burns into my soul
eats discarded babies
allows me to chant razors
& i walked on their paths
& into their jungle
singing songs on independent nights
through the chink in the light
where the alien invaders
storm-troopers & crack vigilantes
twisted my wood into nazi salutes
he freezes by a river of liberty

brute populace daunted i
waltz lengthwise
stride integrity
butter the mountains field
spray howling motifs
gathering flowers trampled
night factory stack
slack the orbit
clamber among debris
shuttered island intransigent
string pearls
gathering dust symphony
symposium's glittering
autonomy rusted
sheets aghast to wind
travel lightly tiptoes
a blocking

casting last tantrums
the glib expression
spun in clay
his mouth motionless
bled by sea-shanties
we led the dictation
it brought him here to rot
in the corpse of our devices
spinning webs' deceit juice of january
there was a call from
at some other moment
his hair turned white and tongue
purple with the rage of doves
spittle rose this ire
catered for in london's blissful cafes
change for twisted hunger
a milk of your blessing
in charge of a thousandth of a curse
he drowned then
in the lure of his own sick

this shark habitat bates with breath
time ordered doodle of lazy shore sundays
time freezes honest platitudes dusk
dark into the castle air (a fringe upon it)
workmen hack and hue & cry
wheeling gulls debauch their masters
a black and white mystery thriller (grabbed by the throat)
emerges from mankind's hanging forest
the toil and threat and sweat and blood
regurgitated ripe over-hangings (kiss curls revisited)
along fault-lines where the stories unfurl
capers on the wind
choice scurries to the victorian almshouses
(the man runs in a circle clucking and clutching)

horn-billed by the throat
encircling slaved cities where (mind)
& madmen muddle by on mandolins (trapped)
walled gardens (secret promises)
we delight in the breath of rancid-gut soldiers
whose (maps) of war resplendent with orchids
blood-red drips capture alsatian times
still (the trains run on time) goblets of steel
hallmarks of last winter's lithe victory
& where the (parable) entered through castle walls
a chink in (remoteness)
factory girls' faces blushed with blood
(rushed) to touch his coat
as he fell before the wall

gliding on gilt-edged promises
the ginger of his hair
reaches down to pick at the bones
buried deep in vaults of desire
carpeted red with corpuscles of profit
& the original motive for murder
grave where she screamed
hoovering of dust & foreign bodies
dangerously down digestive tracts
sauced in a social bile
excavated by journalists
their cries of 'oh, believe us'
twisted in the night

& the politicians' hovel
& midnight of despair
rejecting corporate looseness
in a bar
the tongue twists & unfurls
a licking down of envelopes
'you my dear were always first in my dreams'
the hollowness of what he means
a trumpet plays
a pauper bleeds
day blooms & shakes its bleary
the beard drips ice-cool
along crack-coloured dream-blocks
transubstantiation

## Rages of the Carbolic

a golden-eye of sun blinks
down from mighty tower bocks
along streets heaving masses of molecules
scream into
new fashions the same?
blinkered by definitions
at railway sidings lovers sigh
& part
golden glow of electric hauntings
history books shelved
this discolouration
this badge of honour
he humbly casts before your feet

eyes tear at red-light dawn
traffic-weary victories
a hollow horn blazes
deep into velvet night
following trails upwards
into abandoned hills of love
where we cherished
all that locked within
the thin veil line charity of heart
double-backed and took up the paw-prints
cast upon this anguished i
fool's gold deep buried in past recriminations
it snowed
& the hounds were out among crashing waves
there was always the drowning
sound

# Part 2

**The Other Exploded**

# 1.

igniting craters in gathering blossom
to storms of deluxe transition we ferry
able sea-soldiers subliminally required
a gesture at the foot

breaking fortunes to new requisitions
we gather in harvests of the bland
to dictating new forms of capital explosions
the garden-path is blocked

an extra energy exerts excitement
exhorting byways gathered in the sonnet
a dim-lit lecture betrays new breathing
clutching at the straws

and eventually the clawing diatribe
swallows whole this burble-earth
& new divisions accentuate
rages of the carbolic

## 2.

storm-clouds gather nebular hope
in tectonic plate factories of girth
revealing nature's iconic rolling
forth & froth of pleasures pink & holy
tonight in memory of
a pitch black note forever calling
falling into habits ranged on birchwood
leaning in to listen to the lapping
golden wings expanded laterally
never tires of circular harmonics until
the shopping trip of birth
settles in new borders & peddles
backwards & forwards the ink in the margin
imagine only
where the mark was made

## 3.

stretched taut along the winding
narrow cobbled streets a
string of thoughts precipitated by
the merest tingle
& at the turning
the feet fell in humming harmony
decked out the buttercups
in the glory of some insistent
distant barking & across the bow of breaking
night portraits grown gloomier as a glimmer
of the gossamer painter & musical interludes
the moon-maps of the landscape
jutted by the rutting sea
dissolving sprays in constant leaps
& fortissimos to the shore

## 4.

the leaps and
duty of every
to take this
& imbue with our
it's a quality/& repentant
to sin again would be
yet nightly the sowing by the window
to gather the dusty books
shave off every explanation
& reduce again
this atomic grain

# 5.

crack
the jackdaw
bathes
in the iodine
resplendent castles
capture & capitulate
news waves regurgitate
the slowly sinking mailbags
stuffed with late capital corpses
& stretching long shadows cast
a storm
glimpses in the inkling
such a limbo world of skeleton
rattles in eardrums
a constant stream of
the price of paradise and perdition

## 6.

the willow bends & breaks
to the falling ear
musical scales rejuvenate
a captive to the lyre
& in every doorway the jamb
& emboldment/history's whispering
catcalls & catskins
nine-lives and cat-tails
hawks gather on the moor
lip-reading from the muted mouth
to the spilling of the rutted
the quick of foot & marching
deep furrow on the ridge
exchanging rapid fire
those dogs that barked before
came down to split their joy

# 7.

a clapping in the afterthought
thunderheads such quickening breath
challenges the quiz ink
to borrowers of time replete
& tethering another post
out-landed in the blue beyond
where first our ancestors shook their blood
& fist-fucked villagers whose
lonely jagged tooth
was pulled to the ire of the chief
his ghost whittled bone-down
buried in
the face of
this fair & sceptred isle

## 8.

a rusted nail reaches out resplendent
flesh across the dark & bitter
winds wail against redemption walls
where our hunger came
we chiselled & aggregate
to supplement the mixture
a total creature crawling naked
& split on the hoof
remarkable water-lilies cascade
& dance among the violin creeks
the eddies of this triumphant wind
& time slakes its thirst of men
in their droves along the range
the battlements of a once-tossed rage
which burst this envelope of reason
tricked & battered
with light incisions
of snake-infested funds

## 9.

the bleed chorus of day chopping
at yet another meat-hook verb
estranged way-travellers of night incision
buffeting this eclectic
& haggling of the word
& washing away of its
sore boils and gargoyles
eccentric stones of language
spit grit into his eye
so huge & terrible swapped
with the calling of the birds
whose carrion call & cry we swooped
& rag tail ragamuffin did call us
in the morning trail to come see
where we could offer
something new to be said
beside the statue
& its frozen stare half-eaten

## 10.

he recalled the incident
marked down
by woodcutters
something half-seen
half-drawn
the hanging of
the half-moon
& by the dim lit
backdrop
he says
enter in the small
eerie drips
the splendid droplets
bending to the earth
microbes of language's disfigurement
slithering along the cause
naturally, we blinked
he said we could not believe
what a photograph
was worth

## 11. The Mechanical Recreation of a Rose

petal it stroke
the amulet of chance
i spoke in dance
of chaos frost
& icicle wind to the chant of the living
its breathing
its escaping
from this thorn of keeping
its rhyme a scythe from dreams
it returns
its petal enfolds
the closing of an eye
into hot sensation of a flower
but knot insisting
as such it throttles full mechanical
upon the vine

## 12.

follows stunned silence
around corners at the edge along
byways plunged in future froth
& elements of known
the said exactly pares down
jutting out a bone.

such were the was of past clouds
the credulousness of time its
elements volatile against slashes
the rain of exclamation inside coming
stone dead ends.

sole fever in this moment
its clicking ticking tongue
the measure of the moment
before & now it's gone
a legend in the quagmire
a song for reaching out.

splendid in notation
inferred by each blow limb
the taking of this
required liberty
flattened off the edge.

## 13.

oh for feed the continual
& constant as chiming
its forever settling & increase
from vowels the charming
loop of thought
such staggering degrees
in search of scalding
nemeses to never settle on say
such particulars of birth
as would render sentences to sing
new waves of golden girth

## 14.

an appetite of aeroplanes
songs whistle on the wind
the lilting gesture of generations
fallen to the floor
new exclamations existed
in the aftermath of a glimpse
a fading combing embodiment
stationed on the fire & let
them bleed again to cough
their miracles tiny & resplendent
hitched gaily to the working
in each forgotten form
let them clamber once or more
in the daughters of an alphabet
the fading memory of a regret
once mentioned
never fully formed
nor craven in an image

# 15.

there signed the jewel in bigotry
the room of elephant piquancy
& quite what metaphor entranced
the exit from this site
a wooden castle ensnared
this snake-bit
close around the chortle
referendum of adlib
to mark the houses & salt ash
along the paths of dead
feet at the end of longing
where they trod & flogged
this handsome pig of stuffed legend
atrophy of his skin
the site was mottled and quivering
mole quite torn and shrunken
invited the soldiers into this hovel
infestations of the war
said show them maps & treasure troves
torn from the lid of human waste
sacrifice the burning
a pyre in the wood
the wasted trees of yearning
circled in the jaw

## 16.

yelp less the space of breathe irony
in jaws of emblematic hostility
the battlements gather in storms
a guilt of human whisperings
haunts along such harmony
the shavings

& depth of
in the charging of this changing
the future of this past
rolling debentures/doors/avenues
a lockjaw on your language
a hinge of noun verbs linger
& trail away thru glib filters

the gesture salutes another
& following the frosted finger
its bloody loops
& danger mouth
bit down on rapid
vowel evacuations
a semi-conductor for your electricity
passed thru

each silent

## 17.

this debate degenerates into future hospitality
there among the seas of ruling flotsam tide
a drowning of each individual
like the timeless sunday footballers
who wrench their perfect form of self
& wrap & warp the coming blister shelved
time takes back the words
punctuated by such as this grizzly macabre moon
& the decking out of habit halls
this reason bled & heated a droplet
of the water thru the taps
& the precision of engineering marked
out in maps of social hierarchies
whoever planned the pole from start
to finish & packed the futile hiking shoe
& cleared the ragged path
told me not to wait inherit but position
this darted tongue in leagues of bitumen
& absurd longing for some detoxified air

## 18.

a thirst for
hires up the
riding into town
this memory
this limb
knotted in a dawning
its strength seeps
gathered in the footsteps
at the lights turn
that's where france
joined us at the hip &
birthing pools of childhood things
replenished
they took away our literature
gave us columns of sums
& nouns of mathematics
whispered mass behaving
at ceremonies of the kings
the statue that he made of you
lies rotting in the wind

## 19.

some sleek back dream of ages
reworking clay of language
like asking again at the market
in a strange deluded accent
burst questions into being
from the knot of engraved messages
delivering a corpuscle wrench
to the gut of his opponent
in the stillness of a noun
the night gathers stars around many lives
it wraps them around the tongue
only to burn more lists
forever dying away
a few more seconds lisped
& background days replenished

# Part 3

**The Tapes**

# 1.

first words/the microbe
destiny chapters in freefall
a harmony distorted
in the meaning
the glimpse of
smell this colour
red on black
hatched from a frozen egg
some rarefied belonging
he taps his pencil on the table
aha
& preening his moustache
leans forward into the mirror
cracked
dishevelled
there were others in the atmosphere
a small adjustment to the lapel
      later on a scale of silence/he mouths the nouns
trajectories to right angles
counts the cash/loot/booty
one for me and one for you
as his hunger bleeds

## 2.

from the spaces in-between the rocks
the back & forth of the sea
the humming of illuminations
and in between the reeds

this wind of past regret
flares
glimpses of your flaming-red
& locks

he looks at his watch
& scans the beach
a melancholic shell lingers

the dribbling from his tongue
& acid dripping from these eyes
the words are only shapes

in the distance

between

this cognition
& the next

letter

## 3.

spider scurries
across the stains
and at the foot of
our statue
i glimpse
the space of sky
the typewriter with the broken a key
& that blank piece of paper

he never mourned for you
skin of his skin
the cool breath now left
& only the fan whirring

yesterday &&&&&&&&&&&&&
alan recalls recoiling from the french kiss
he gave to his aunt by mistake

& your underwear over the radiator
reminders that your feet once touched
similar vibrations

he had not gone into the spare room since that time
but across the hall he can hear the rise &fall

of

## 4.

an exciting series of runs/at the oval
in human waves against/the iraqi lines

the thin white line blinks on the screen

he opened his mouth
but there was no

a white picket fence against
your white picket face fenced
in

outside it is raining
beetles on the lawn
if you want to know how the girl will turn out

      on your tongue the tantalizing taste
      is something sweet & sour
      how you remember bedtime stories

wrapped in your blanket
field of dreams
behind the whites of your eyes
symbiotic fluid leaks

& all the kings horses and all the kings men
marching an army of dreams on its belly
into the umbilical

## 5.

jutting out to sea the rock
& lapping gently
back & forth
the beam searches across horizons
your beacon
turns amber in our dreams
where i entered into
the question mark
the sifting
fog & the smearing
was his face faded against

                          they said to leave the grave unmarked

but a stain on his pillow
& the failing alphabet
he struggles to find

                      exactly the right words to say

what fitted together
& kept us from the frozen
up on the cliffs
away from his searching eye
from blue & black this rolling tongue will not still

it goes on & on swallowing hope

## 6.

i is at the casting word
the shadow of its meaning
cloaked in rusting

& it dismembers
at junctions of memory
membranes of the neuron

jammed into the idle socket
one eye on such meaning
as can trace along his spine

                      the pen spirographs
                      into isotopes
                      they marched the prisoners

& then back again
here's your howling alphabet
on the ward in tatters
its spluttering ...

seeps into/war wounds

# Part 4

End Poems

# A.

& between the hairline crack
that enabled
when you were born
& later spinning around
& around
calling for something wild to protect yourself
your mama and your papa
came in from the sea & said today another
but quickly you reverted
back into the corner of
the holy order & never said
& we had to guess which insect
& later which mammal
& when we said human
there was just the laughter
it was just your joke you said
& got out the maps & said i name these countries
& later we named the shapes of natural disasters
& you said my god we killed them all!

# B. iiiiiiii

shot thru the plastic
confines & the corner of the angle
where your mouth drool
& the consequence of judge tongue
lip & dressing of the sentence
out into the secular city
cold with only cloth of sound-bite
& jargon of the pool where he fell
the cops & nouns gather
in the final glimmer of how we feel

## C. Islington Poem

trapped beneath the feet/political sewers
infamous tony blair & tiny hairs
& bloody ink gutters run between
the hampstead & highgate express
& the islington gazette
cerebral supporters of the arsenal
lenin & jeremy corbyn
(together on one recording)
they bleed their
sweet neurons nightly
magnificently on the balcony
geordie armstrong on the wing
& a seething mass of white irish
the smell of bertie mee
& charlie george years later
the neverending buzz of arsene wenger
the wheels of the crush
recalled the speeches they made
the royal woolwich & marches
bands at the angel pub
roughly sleeping
the wheels of the crush
prisoners of the sex trade
the boys and girls
the girls and boys

layered in sinful alliance
ghostly gods and goddesses
their bricked-in luxury apartments
the town hall clock
divisions of temple money
& we ofwords
ourbanners flared against parliamentary democracy
& we do not support
the wheels of the crush
our tongues inflamed in irons of welt & stone
& highbury
& the graves of our traitors
below these city streets

(you cannot meet us)
we are beyond your expectations

## D. Tears Trace Down

the bottled language

compressed in the phial & now
injected into his capillaries

from the moment he was born
just the ampersands

& the hollow mouth melting
into ego's i shadows

blood leaking & congealed
from the corners of his mind

a freshlyminted verb
hooks onto the tongue

which fails

# E. Steve's Journey

at all this dysfunction --- function
he trod (from) dislocation the strand
lolling on his tongue
a tantalizing
paragraph
(shorn)

he walked on
not (once) in harmony
projectiles on the periphery
a stolen moment
(from where the shards of grass)

moments melting in the weeds
(his eye glued to the door)
from where his footsteps came
his shadow (a patchwork)
cast into future domains

a spittle of language surrounded him
                                      trapped him in the gauze
new housing developments splintered
into this vast & hostile swamp of nouns
the guard noticed in doggerel
the swift-release of adrenaline alsations – to silence seething
pavements

www.ingramcontent.com/pod-product-compliance
Lightning Source LLC
Chambersburg PA
CBHW051703040426
42446CB00009B/1279